Children of the World

Finland

For their help in the preparation of *Children of the World: Finland*, the editors gratefully thank Employment and Immigration Canada, Ottawa, Ont.; the US Immigration and Naturalization Service, Washington, DC; the Embassy of Finland (US), Washington, DC; the International Institute of Wisconsin, Milwaukee; the United States Department of State, Bureau of Public Affairs, Office of Public Communication, Washington, DC, for unencumbered use of material in the public domain; and Carita Heid, Sonja Varpiainen, and Hannu Varpiainen, Milwaukee.

Library of Congress Cataloging-in-Publication Data

Bjener, Tamiko.
   Finland.

   (Children of the world)
   Bibliography: p.
   Includes index.
   Summary: Describes the life of a boy in Rovaniemi, the capital of Finnish Lapland, who dreams of being a pilot, and discusses Finland's ethnic groups, religion, government, education, industry, geography, and history.
   1. Finland — Social life and customs — Juvenile literature. 2. Children — Finland — Juvenile literature. [1. Finland — Social life and customs. 2. Family life — Finland.]
I. Knowlton, MaryLee, 1946-
II. Sachner, Mark, 1948-   . III. Title. IV. Series:
Children of the world (Milwaukee, Wis.)
DL1017.B54   1988   J 948.97   87-42580
ISBN 1-55532-293-3
ISBN 1-55532-218-2 (lib. bdg.)

North American edition first published in 1988 by

Gareth Stevens, Inc.
7317 West Green Tree Road   Milwaukee, Wisconsin 53223, USA

Typeset by Ries Graphics ltd., Milwaukee.
Design: Laurie Bishop and Laurie Shock.
Map design: Gary Moseley.

1   2   3   4   5   6   7   8   9   92   91   90   89   88

Children of the World

Finland

Photography by
Tamiko Bjener

Edited by
MaryLee Knowlton &
Mark J. Sachner

Gareth Stevens Publishing
Milwaukee

. . . a note about *Children of the World*:

The children of the world live in fishing towns, Arctic regions, and urban centers, on islands and in mountain valleys, on sheep ranches and fruit farms. This series follows one child in each country through the pattern of his or her life. Candid photographs show the children with their families, at school, at play, and in their communities. The text describes the dreams of the children and, often through their own words, tells how they see themselves and their lives.

Each book also explores events that are unique to the country in which the child lives, including festivals, religious ceremonies, and national holidays. The *Children of the World* series does more than tell about foreign countries. It introduces the children of each country and shows readers what it is like to be a child in that country.

. . . and about *Finland*:

Tuomas lives in Rovaniemi, the capital of Finnish Lapland. Located directly on the Arctic Circle, Rovaniemi is known for its severe winters. But life on the Arctic Circle is also fun, and summers are quite pleasant. Tuomas enjoys living in the Arctic regions, and he dreams of becoming a pilot after college so he can travel and meet people from other parts of the world.

To enhance this book's value in libraries and classrooms, comprehensive reference sections include up-to-date data about Finland's geography, demographics, language, currency, education, culture, industry, and natural resources. *Finland* also features a bibliography, research topics, activity projects, and discussions of such subjects as Helsinki, the country's history, political system, ethnic and religious composition, and language.

The living conditions and experiences of children in Finland vary tremendously according to economic, environmental, and ethnic circumstances. The reference sections help bring to life for young readers the diversity and richness of the culture and heritage of Finland. Of particular interest are discussions of the Laplanders, or Sami, a native culture that has made its presence felt in the language and traditions of Finland.

CONTENTS

Tuomas' family: Pauliina, Emilia, Ilkka, Tuomas, Kaarina.

Hei! Minun nimeni on Tuomas Miikka Taneli Ikäheimo

"Hi! My name is Tuomas Miikka Taneli Ikäheimo

LIVING IN FINLAND:
Tuomas, a Boy from the Arctic Circle

Meet Tuomas Ikäheimo of Finland — known as Suomi to the Finns. He lives in the northern area of Finland, called Lapland, in the city of Rovaniemi. Rovaniemi is on the edge of the Arctic Circle. Though it was nearly destroyed by the Germans during World War II, Rovaniemi today is a modern city of over 30,000 people and the capital of Finnish Lapland. Lapland, sometimes

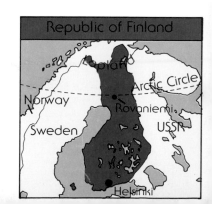

Republic of Finland

spelled *Lappland,* is also the name of the larger region that includes parts of Norway, Sweden, Finland, and the USSR.

Tuomas is 12 years old. He lives with his father, Ilkka; his mother, Kaarina; and his sisters, 17-year-old Pauliina and eight-year-old Emilia. Their house is on the River Kemi, the longest river in Finland, about ten minutes by bike from downtown Rovaniemi. The River Kemi is wonderful for swimming and boating in the summer. In the winter Tuomas and his family enjoy skating, sledding, and cross-country skiing on the river and in the wilderness areas around it.

Lapland is mostly wilderness with lakes and deciduous forests. Here reindeer, elk, arctic fox, and many other animals live. It is so far north that from May through July the sun never sets. All night long, it is light enough to read.

Tuomas' family inherited this house from his grandparents. They remodeled it three years ago.

8

Finland's largest river, the Kemi, flows past the front of Tuomas' house.

Tuomas' Family

Tuomas' parents were married while they were in college. Ilkka worked on a sightseeing boat while he was in law school. Today he is a lawyer with a small firm in town. He drives from one place to another to handle traffic accidents, divorces, and other legal cases. His car is a Saab. It is 10 years old and has a faulty handbrake. Kaarina worries that it will break down in the middle of the forest, but Illka is very attached to it. He says the engine is good enough. Both Tuomas and his sister Pauliina can drive. But they still take lessons from their father on private roads.

Tuomas' father's office. In the summer, Tuomas meets his father here for lunch almost every day.

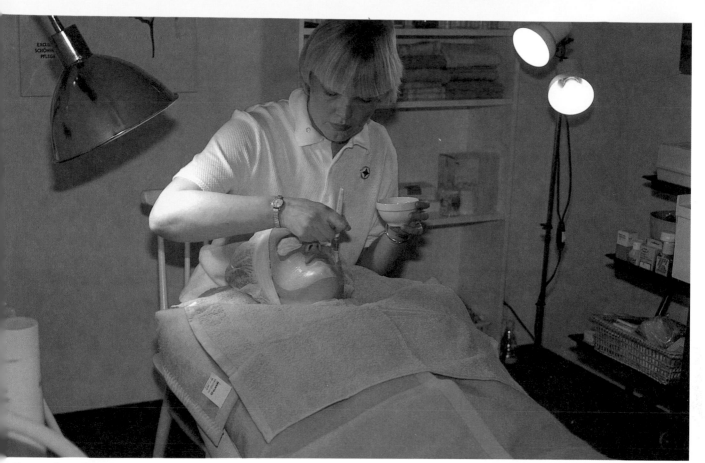
Tuomas' mother does a facial in her beauty salon.

Kaarina runs a beauty shop in the basement of their house. She does facials and herbal massages. When she is working, the children help prepare meals and clean the house. The children have become very cooperative since their mother began working. She thinks the responsibilities are good for them.

Tuomas' family has just remodeled their living room. The furniture is a mixture of modern and traditional design.

Inside, the Ikäheimo house is very modern. Finnish designers and architects are well-known throughout the world. Light wood, brightly colored fabrics, and simple lines are typical of the Finnish look. When Finnish designers manufacture a product, they are concerned with how well something works as well as how good it looks.

The children think a great deal about what they want to do when they grow up. Pauliina is thinking about leaving home. She is saving money to go to medical school in Canada after she graduates from high school.

Tuomas is perfectly happy where he is. He wants to be a pilot after he graduates from college. He hopes to meet people from many countries and learn different customs. But he wants his home base to be Rovaniemi. Emilia is thinking about her future, too. She can't decide whether to be a beautician in her mother's shop or a flight attendant on her brother's plane.

Tuomas and Emilia wash the dishes and let them dry by themselves in the cabinet.

Tuomas and Emilia watch the news on TV with Ilkka.

13

A Finnish Meal

Now that the children are getting older, someone is always missing at suppertime. Tonight Emilia is having supper at a friend's house. She misses a very lively conversation about her sister's hair.

At 17, Pauliina is eager to show her independence. Today she came home with her hair very short and orange. Her mother was stunned into silence. Her father took out a picture of her with long hair and kissed it. Tuomas thinks her hair looks great! By suppertime, her parents are getting used to it, especially since she told them the orange will wash out in a few days.

Who will be the first to break up? Everyone tries hard not to be too silly at the table!

Supper is a light meal because the family will get together again before bed to talk about their day over tea and sandwiches. Kaarina makes simple suppers for anyone who shows up. Sometimes she makes salmon soup with potatoes and onions and cream. Other times she makes *Karjalanpiirakka,* a kind of bread filled with rice and topped with a spread made from butter and hard-boiled eggs. The family loves desserts — baked cloudberries and cream and *Raparperi,* a sweet-and-sour rhubarb dish.

Finns eat lots of fish. They prepare it deep-fried, or rolled and baked, or in a vinegar sauce. Dark bread, *Näkkileipa* (hard bread), and cheese are parts of every Finnish meal.

The most famous dish of Lapland is reindeer. Tuomas' family often eats smoked reindeer meat on slices of bread. Cooked or broiled like beef, it is served with a sweet lingonberry jam.

The children's favorite — a thin pancake with cloudberry jam.

Fried reindeer meat with lingonberry jam.

Karjalanpiirakka, a special bread dish.

An Evening at Home

After school and in the evenings, the family spends time together or with friends. Pauliina is often out, but she returns in time to chat before bed. When their father is out of town overnight, the children play together. When he's home, they watch television. Their mother likes to read rather than watch TV. Tuomas is much like her. He sometimes spends the evening in his room reading and listening to music on his headphones.

All the children have their own bedrooms. Tuomas has modern furniture and posters of his favorite rock stars. The bright colors and clean lines of his furniture and bedding are typically Finnish. Their lightness is cheerful during the long winter.

Tuomas' room.

Tuomas' school supplies.

Emilia's room. Her furniture has been in the family for over 100 years.

At night, Tuomas reads or listens to tapes before he goes to sleep.

Emilia's bedroom has furniture that has been in her mother's family for over 100 years. It belonged to Kaarina when she was a little girl. Some day, it will go to one of Kaarina's grandchildren.

Tuomas' parents are raising their children to appreciate the past as well as the future. Their house and home life are a mix of old and new. Sometimes Tuomas and Pauliina think their parents are too old-fashioned. But the family talks about their feelings and ideas and everybody learns from each other.

A church in Rovaniemi. After much of the town was destroyed during World War II, Rovaniemi was redesigned as a modern city. Today, no building may be built more than five stories high.

Downtown Rovaniemi.

Sweets and more sweets!

Summer!

It's summertime. The children are out of school and have lots of free time. Today Tuomas is getting a haircut. Like most Finnish children, he has his hair cut in the latest style.

After his haircut, Tuomas stops to visit his uncle's lumber mill and factory. The lumber is precisely measured and cut before being assembled into furniture.

On his way to a stylish haircut.

Tuomas' uncle's factory, where furniture and toys are made.

The family visits Tuomas' cousin, Peter. Peter and his family live outside town, deep in the forest. The children love to come for a day or a week. The countryside entertains the children in many ways.

The blueberries are ripe! Tuomas and Emilia spend the morning picking them. They'll have them with milk for breakfast, lunch, and dinner for as long as they are in season. The mosquitoes and gnats are fierce around the bushes. What started out as fun ends in a flurry of slapping and scratching.

Tuomas plays with Ami, his cousin's dog. He'd love to have a dog of his own, but his mother is allergic to them.

Picking clusters of blueberries. When they're ripe, blueberries make great juice and jam.

The ripe blueberries are big, sweet, and juicy.

Tuomas with Peter's dog, Ami.

A special summer treat: out for a spin in his cousin's very own car!

Tuomas and Peter practice their archery. Peter is very good, especially for a little kid. He gives Tuomas tips.

Now for what Tuomas loves best about visiting Peter — driving around the country roads in Peter's car. Lapland has many isolated areas, so many children learn to drive quite early. Tuomas sometimes drives his parents' Saab on private roads. When he visits his relatives outside of town, Tuomas is especially anxious to drive Peter's own little car.

Practicing archery on a weekend visit.

Cloudberries are a special summer product from Lapland.

Tuomas keeps his eye on the ball.

Soccer, one of Tuomas' many sports.

Tuomas watches in anticipation as the ball heads for the basket.

Summer Sports and Fun

Summer is the time for outdoor sports. Tuomas loves many of them, but he's best at tennis. Today Tuomas can't wait for his father to come home. He meets him at his office after work, and they play till late in the evening under the summer sun.

Tomorrow is a tennis tournament, and Tuomas will compete in the junior division. The first time he competed, he was very tense. His father gave him some advice — sports are to be enjoyed. Since then he has relaxed and become a very good tennis player.

22

Pauliina plays *pesäpallo,* a Finnish version of baseball. Pesäpallo is based on North American baseball, and there are many similarities between pesäpallo and its North American version. The diamond is certainly the same. But there are some variations, too. One of the most interesting is this: In pesäpallo, the pitcher does not stand on a pitcher's mound. Instead, he or she faces the batter only two or three yards (or meters) away and throws the ball straight up in the air. The batter tries to hit the ball as it falls. Often on summer evenings the whole family goes to games to cheer Pauliina on.

As summer draws to an end, the days become shorter. Here on the border of the Arctic Circle, the North Pole doesn't seem very far away. In fact, even in summer, you can find Santa Claus in Lapland! Tourists are always glad to see him, and he's around Lapland all year round.

A game of pesäpallo played around 8:00 p.m.

A late-summer photo session with Santa at the North Pole Lodge.

23

Tuomas' class. It's 1:00 on an August afternoon, and already the shadows are getting long.

The school grounds.

The Start of a New School Year

The Rantavitikan Primary School is where Tuomas and his sister Emilia go to school. Their father went to school here, too. The school was founded in 1870 and was one of the few buildings to survive when the Germans moved through the city. It's just a five minute walk from Tuomas' house.

Concentrating in class.

A 6th grade science textbook.

Tuomas is in the 6th grade. His class has 25 students. The new term starts in mid August, and Tuomas and his friends are glad to see each other after two months of vacation. School starts at 8:00 a.m.

At the start of the school term all the students receive the textbooks they'll be using this year. On top of the excitement of the first day of school, Tuomas' class has a substitute teacher. The regular teacher, Mr. Savolainen, has not yet returned from his vacation in Spain. Mr. Tero, the substitute, is a university student who has been substitute teaching for three years. The students know him and respect him, and he smiles at their excitement on the first day of school.

The day is noisy and lively, but by midmorning, things are settling down.

Everybody pays close attention to Mr. Tero, their substitute teacher.

As in classrooms around the world, the first day of the new term is spent discussing summer vacation. Tuomas tells about a visit to the North Pole Lodge, where materials from Arctic explorations and Lapland culture are shown. His friend Timo talks about his days hunting and fishing with his father at a mountain cabin. Finns cherish their summers. Many have summer homes outside the cities where they spend the warm summer months.

Lunch is delivered to Tuomas' school and eaten right in the classrooms.

Rice porridge topped with fruit soup and hard bread with smoked meat.

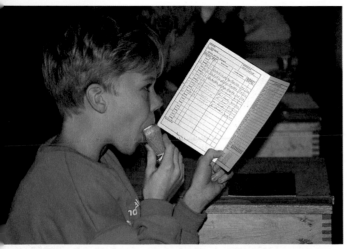

In Tuomas' class, the teacher hands out ice cream cones and report cards at the same time!

The students have Finnish and English classes before lunch. English starts in the 3rd grade. Tuomas still finds it very difficult.

School lunches are free. The students help carry the food in from the kitchen. In most Finnish schools, the children eat in cafeterias. But Tuomas' school is very old, and lunch is actually delivered to the school. The students begin meals with a prayer. Most Finns are Lutheran. They study religion in school and have hymn-singing assemblies on Friday afternoons.

After lunch the students play in the schoolyard before settling down again to math and science classes.

Physical education. The students get as much exercise during recess as they do in gym class!

Tuomas' father wakes him up each morning for school.

School in Winter

The first term passes quickly, and fall turns to winter. The day starts out dark, cold, and early. Tuomas puts on several layers of clothes.

He checks the temperature before he goes. If it's too cold, they'll have to stay in for recess at school. Today is December 17, and the temperature is -13°F (-25°C). The sun hasn't been seen since November.

The layered look, Finnish style!

Getting dressed in winter, layer by layer.

Ready for the cold: outerwear and boots in the school corridor.

Another class picture. This one was taken at 1:00 on a December afternoon, when the sun is still below the horizon.

The school grounds in winter.

The weather is fair today. The sky is pink above the distant tree tops. The children assemble outside for a class picture with Mr. Savolainen, their regular teacher.

31

The Rovaniemi City Library. It's a pleasant place for studying and reading after school.

Bibles and textbooks share shelf space in the classroom.

A winter scene, by Tuomas.

This afternoon the students rehearse the Christmas show they will be putting on for their parents. They will be singing songs from the *Kalevala*, a collection of old folk songs and poetry.

Tuomas and his classmates are dressed for their roles. Their play is based on stories from the *Kalevala*. Tuomas seems to have landed a major part!

The play goes well. Tuomas often reads from a book of *Old Kalevala* he got for his birthday. These songs and poems are special to him, and he's happy his class is using them for the Christmas show. They help him understand the world of Finnish myths and the lives and thoughts of people long ago.

The class Christmas party.

Shoveling snow is Tuomas' main chore around the house in winter.

Other Winter Activity

Tuomas is a good student. On a scale of 4 to 10, he gets nines in all his subjects: Finnish, math, history, science, geography, physical education, music, art, and English. He knows he'll go on to college, but he doesn't know yet what he'll study. He says it will be something in math or the sciences.

Life doesn't slow down in winter. The children study and read more than in summer, but they're still outdoors as much as they can be. Many of the children's household chores take place outdoors. Tuomas shovels the snow, and Emilia helps with the laundry. On Saturdays Emilia's job is to hang the quilts, pillows, and rugs out to air.

Tuomas loves working with computers. His friend Timo has one at home that Tuomas often uses. Sometimes he can use the one at his father's office. Winter is a good time for this kind of work. It's certainly better than helping Emilia with the laundry!

Tuomas enjoys working — and playing — at his friend's personal computer.

Emilia takes bed linens and rugs to air out on the snow.

The River Kemi is frozen over. Tuomas and his father play hockey in front of the house. The family often goes skiing on slopes near the house. They love both downhill and cross-country skiing.

Tuomas plays ice hockey with his father.

Ounasvaara ski slope, about a 15-minute drive from Tuomas' house.

The bus station in downtown Rovaniemi. These pictures were taken at about 1:00 in the afternoon — another sunless winter day on the Arctic Circle.

The walk home from school.

Since the sun does not rise, the sky is dark all day long. But this is no problem for sports lovers. The slopes and rinks in Rovaniemi are lit up brightly all day.

In the half-daylight of the afternoon, the snow-encased landscape presents an eerie, beautiful picture.

Downtown Rovaniemi is crowded with Christmas shoppers.

Christmas in Finnish Lapland

Christmas is coming and there's lots to do. The whole family has been cooking and shopping for weeks. The children put the finishing touches on the tree. Some people still cut their Christmas trees in the forest, but they are also sold in town.

A photo with Santa at the North Pole Lodge.

Decorating the tree.

A special moment with Santa and a reindeer.

A special treat for Tuomas is a visit to Santa Claus — not unusual in Western countries.

What is unusual, though, is the ride in his reindeer-driven sleigh. That could only happen in Lapland.

The sauna on Christmas Eve.

On Christmas Eve day no one has to tell Tuomas to get up. His job is to fill buckets with water. In a few hours the water will freeze except in the middle. He will pour out the unfrozen water and light candles in the cavity it leaves. All around the town neighbors will do the same, and the lights will twinkle throughout the day and evening.

When all the preparations for tomorrow are done, the family goes to light candles at the family gravesites. Many people visit the cemetery to honor their ancestors at Christmastime.

Preparing the iced candle holders.

A visit to the family gravesite.

Tuomas' relatives gather at his house on Christmas Day. His grandmother is in the center of this family picture.

Salmon.

Christmas nuts.

Christmas porridge.

Christmas ham and laatikko.

Christmas pastry.

Reindeer meat.

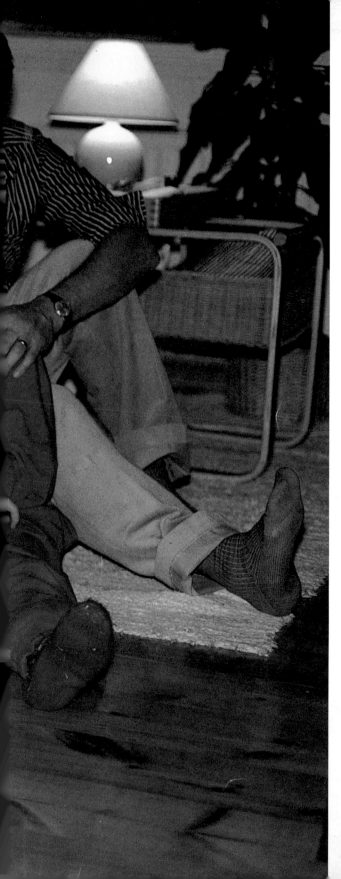

The whole family gathers beneath the Christmas tree. Tuomas hopes for this kind of peace forever.

After Christmas dinner, Tuomas and his sisters go to their rooms. In the family tradition, now is the time Santa will come. For now, all the children are believers.

When they hear the door slam, they rush out and find their gifts under the tree. It is a happy, warm time for the family.

Tuomas with all his Christmas gifts. Just looking at them makes him happy!

Asla's mother weaves an old family design into their clothing.

Asla (standing) and his family.

Dinner time.

The Sami: Asla, Another Boy from Lapland

Asla is a 13-year-old boy from Ivalo Village, in the far north. He and his family are Lapps, or Sami, an ancient people who live in the northern reaches of Finland, Sweden, Norway, and the USSR. They are very proud of their culture, and they keep many traditions alive today. One of these is their clothing. It is made by hand and adorned with family designs.

Asla wants to be a reindeer breeder, like his father. Since his school is far from home, he lives in a dormitory during the school year. During vacations, he goes out with his father in the fields and over the hills camping and hunting reindeer. His father is teaching him all about raising reindeer. He knows how to lasso a reindeer, how to use knives and guns, and how to fish.

The Sami use reindeer for tourism, racing, and pulling sleighs. Reindeer meat is eaten in many forms. Their fur is used to make coats, gloves, and boots. Their bones are used for knitting needles and their brains for yeast for bread. Asla's parents made a cradle out of reindeer hide for their son when he was born.

Hay inside reindeer-hide boots: perfect insulation!

Nowadays, snowmobiles often replace reindeer sleighs.

A baby cradle made out of reindeer hide. At home it's a cradle. Outside, it's a tiny sled.

Most Sami do not own land, so they measure their wealth by how many reindeer they own. It is considered very rude to ask a Sami how many reindeer he has, just as it would be rude to ask someone how much money she has in the bank.

Children are often given baby reindeer to raise. The baby is marked with the child's own mark, and the child looks out for it. Asla has a baby reindeer. Its mother was killed by a wolf, and the baby depends on Asla for its survival. Like children everywhere, Asla loves animals. His pet just happens to be a reindeer.

FOR YOUR INFORMATION: Finland

Official name: Republic of Finland
Suomi (soo-WAH-mee)

Capital: Helsinki

History

Early History — the Sami and the Finns

The earliest Finns settled in Finland around 100 AD. They were tribes living in the forests that surrounded lakes. Many scholars believe they once lived in what is now west-central Siberia. Even before they came, the Lapps, or Sami as they are known in their own language, were living in the north tracking the reindeer across Norway, Sweden, Finland, and Russia. It is estimated that the Sami moved into the area after the last ice age, which ended about 10,000 years ago.

Finland under Sweden...

Swedish settlers out for the crusades made Finland a part of Sweden in 1154. Sweden was a powerful country in the following centuries. It expanded in all directions. Finland was a rich source of soldiers for Sweden's military campaigns,

The center of Helsinki, Finland's capital city.

and many were lost in foreign countries. In 1696-97 a famine killed about one-third of the Finnish population.

. . .and Russia

War from 1700-1721 ended Sweden's rule as a world power. While Sweden was busy defending itself in Europe, Russia began to take over in Finland. Throughout the 18th century, Russia either occupied Finland or demanded land in return for withdrawing. By 1809, Russia was occupying Finland and did not intend to leave. Sweden was forced to let Russia make Finland part of Russia.

Under Russia, Finland enjoyed a great deal of autonomy. National pride and identity developed, and Finnish became a national language. Finns stopped thinking of themselves as Swedes. At the same time, they resisted thinking of themselves as Russians. For its part, however, Russia was increasingly thinking of Finland as part of Russia. Toward the end of the 19th century national pride in Finland grew as Russian repression increased. In 1917, shortly after the Russian Revolution, Finland declared its independence. A short but bitter civil war followed in 1918 between Finnish nationalists and Finns who wanted to stay Russian. Today the government is a coalition of Finns of both political leanings.

World War II — A Dilemma for Finland

When World War II broke out Finland was in a bad position. Initially it tried to remain neutral, like the other Scandinavian countries. However, when the USSR tried to annex, or add, parts of northeast Finland for its own defense, Finland allied itself with Nazi Germany. As the USSR had feared, Germany used Finland as a base for attacking the Soviet frontier. Finland would pay dearly for its alliance. When it became clear that the USSR was going to win the war in that area, Finland stopped fighting and negotiated a peace in Moscow. The Finnish government agreed to pay large fines and to give up some territory in the north. They had to pay the USSR over 500 million dollars and resettle 400,000 people from the territories that were no longer Finland's.

The War and After

The war with the USSR was over. However, there were still German troops in the north of Finland. They would not leave voluntarily, so Finland had to drive them out. As they left, the German troops destroyed most of what they passed through — forests, villages, and cities. From November of 1939 to spring of 1945, while Finland was at war with either the USSR or Germany, 100,000 Finnish soldiers were killed. Today a treaty with the USSR states that Finland will not permit its land to be used as a base for attacking the USSR, and the two countries have key trade relations.

Finns take great pride in knowing that except for Great Britain and the USSR, Finland was the only European country to avoid foreign occupation during World War II. Although the Germans did attack or enter these three countries, they did not set up an occupation force to rule the people. An additional source of pride for Finns is that while Germany forced countries throughout Europe to deport their Jewish citizens to be killed, Finnish Jews remained safe at home.

Population and Ethnic Groups

Most likely, present-day Finns are descended from the Sami who moved into the region after the Great Ice Age, which ended about 10,000 years ago, and from immigrants who arrived between 100 and 800 AD. They usually have blue or gray eyes and blond or light brown hair.

Two minority groups also live in Finland. The Lapps, or Sami, live in the northern area known as Lapland. Once they traveled across the tops of Norway, Sweden, Finland, and Russia, following the reindeer. Today international borders confine them to the country in which they happen to live. About 5,000 of them live in Finland. The second, less well-known minority group is the Gypsies. About 5,500 Gypsies live in south Finland.

The population of Finland is about 4.8 million. The growth rate is slow. About 5% of the population emigrates, mostly to Sweden. The birth rate is low. Because of the low rate of growth, the government offers benefits to families with children. Each family, regardless of income, gets an allowance for each child. It can be used for child care or to help support a family while one parent stays home to care for the children. Or the money can be used to pay for the children's college education if they go somewhere other than Finland's free universities.

Government

Finland is a parliamentary republic. The highest offices are the presidency and the one-house parliament. In 1906, Finnish women became the first in Europe to vote. Unlike in other countries, women also became members of parliament, cabinet ministers, and ambassadors in the early part of the century.

The parliament is made up of members of many political parties. The make-up of the parliament changes each four years as elections are held, but the government is basically stable. Though the parties have strongly-held differences because some are communist or socialist and others are conservative, they tend to be held in balance. The conservatives have gained in recent years as the economy grows strong. The communists have lost some of their influence as their intended supporters flourish under a capitalist economy.

Finland has an extremely high standard of living. Most Finnish families have TV sets, cars, and many appliances, and many city-dwellers also have country homes.

Finland's wealth is among the most evenly distributed in the industrial world. These facts have this effect: most people in Finland live quite well.

Finland is a neutral country that has warm relations with many countries around the world. Its main purpose in its dealings with other countries is to keep itself secure and independent. This is especially true of its relations with the USSR, with whom Finland shares a border. Finland's relations with other countries are based primarily on trade, tourism, and cultural exchanges. Since 1955, it has supported and participated in the United Nations' efforts to find peaceful solutions to disputes and to help develop the independence of Third World countries.

Currency

Finnish currency is the *markka* and the *penni*. One markka equals 100 penni.

Language

Finland has two official languages, Finnish and Swedish. Finnish is the first language of 93.6% of the people; 6.2% speak Swedish; and 0.2% speak something else. Finnish is not like any of the other Scandinavian languages. It is one of the Finno-Ugrian languages, a group of Asian languages. It is related to Hungarian. Lappish, the language of the Sami, is also Finno-Ugrian.

In school, children study in the language they speak at home. Newspapers, government papers, and educational materials are in both languages. In bilingual areas, streets signs are also in both Finnish and Swedish. When children are in 3rd grade, they are required to study English. They must also learn either Swedish or Finnish, whichever they do not speak at home.

Religion

About 90% of Finland is Lutheran. Children learn religion in the public schools as part of their coursework. The church is allowed to tax its members.

Education

Children from seven to sixteen are required to go to school, and almost 100% of Finns can read. From 1st through 6th grades, they study these subjects: religious knowledge, environmental studies, Finnish and Swedish, English, history and social studies, civics, math, biology, geography, physical education, music, art, and handicrafts. Finnish schools offer children many chances to study foreign languages. Many children graduate speaking four or more languages.

The school day usually goes from 8:00 a.m. to 3:00 p.m. The noon meal is free. Vacations come around Christmas, for 10 weeks in the summer, and in late February for a week of skiing. The school system also has summer camps for children's recreation. This gives city children a chance to live in the country during the summer. Children go to either a Finnish or Swedish speaking camp.

Education is free through the university level. After grade school, children may either drop out or go on to high school in either a vocational or academic program. Most go on. Enrollment in high school is the highest in the world. One in four children in Finland graduates from one of Finland's nine universities.

The Arts

Literature and the Kalevala

During the centuries Finland was under Swedish rule, Swedish was the official language and Finnish was only a spoken language. The major literary works were all written in Swedish. In the 19th century, Finns began to feel Finnish. A loose organization of artists and thinkers came together. They helped develop a Finnish sense of identity for their people that was independent of Russia and Sweden. One of these writers, Elias Lönnrot, began collecting songs, poems, and tales from Finnish folklore. He organized them into one long literary work called the *Kalevala,* which he published in 1835. The *Kalevala* became an important base for Finnish culture, a poem of 22,795 lines in its second edition, published in 1849. It has been translated into more than 35 languages.

The material of the *Kalevala* is very old. It reflects ancient beliefs and accounts of the creation and history of the world passed down through song and story from one generation to the next. The stories, poems, and songs that Lönnrot used were about a mighty singer and magician named Väinämöinen and his friend, the blacksmith, Ilmarinen. They forged the Sampo, with which they performed great feats of magic and strength. The Sampo was a tool that changed form from one poem or tale to another. But it always had magical powers and was a symbol of good luck and power.

Music and Theater

The material Lönnrot collected in the *Kalevala* came to him in the form of songs known as *runot.* One song is a *runo,* or *rune* in English. Because they had all been learned by word of mouth, many songs and stories came in different forms and with different melodies. They were performed by a singer called a runo singer. These songs were learned from the singer's parents. There were famous runo singer families. These families made changes in songs over the generations, adding to them, combining songs, and changing tunes. It was not important to keep the songs the same. In fact, they were meant to change. The selection of songs of a good runo singer was very large. Some knew over 11,000 lines of poetry that they could sing or fashion into new songs.

The singers were accompanied by a stringed instrument called the *kantele*, known as the Finnish harp. The kantele is a popular instrument even today. It looks something like a zither or an autoharp. The player either holds the instrument on his or her lap or places it on a table.

Today folk music is very important in Finland. Summer folk music festivals throughout the country keep the traditional music alive. At these festivals people listen to music and learn new ways of singing and playing old songs.

Folk music has also influenced serious music in Finland. The work of composer Jean Sibelius draws many melodies and themes from Finnish folk songs. His famous *Finlandia*, first performed in 1899, was greatly inspiring to the Finnish people who recognized in it melodies from their folk heritage. The premier performance of *Finlandia* coincided with increasingly repressive actions on the part of Russia. Following the performance, the people took to the streets in open demonstration of Finnish pride.

Music and theater in Finland are both very popular. Both draw on traditional Finnish forms and on European influences. Finns love jazz and hold an international jazz festival annually in Pori. The Finnish National Theatre was founded in 1872. Today there are 50 professional theaters in Finland with 2.5 million spectators a year. These theaters are subsidized, or supported, by public funding. The Finnish theater shows much Russian influence in acting and directing style, but its favorite playwright is Shakespeare.

Finnish Architecture and Design

Finland's artistic influence has been most widely felt in architecture and design. Around the turn of the century architects Alvar Aalto and Eliel Saarinen began to develop their art and philosophy. They also began to design buildings. Their influence has been worldwide. Saarinen spent much of his life as director of the Cranbrook Academy of Art in Bloomfield Hills, Michigan. In the United States, Aalto designed buildings from Boston to Oregon. His glass and furniture designs are in the Museum of Modern Art in New York City. They are familiar even to people who don't know who designed them. The Finnish design tradition, like those of other Scandinavian countries, embraces many forms. Designers and architects often overlap in their work, designing both the structure of a building and what goes inside as well — textiles, furniture, and dishes.

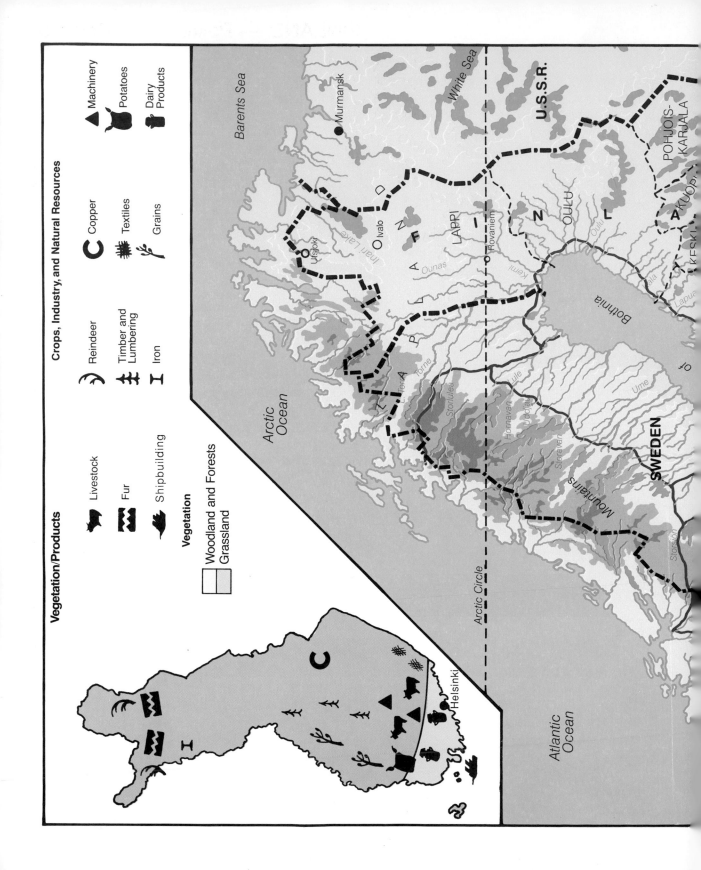

FINLAND — Political and Physical

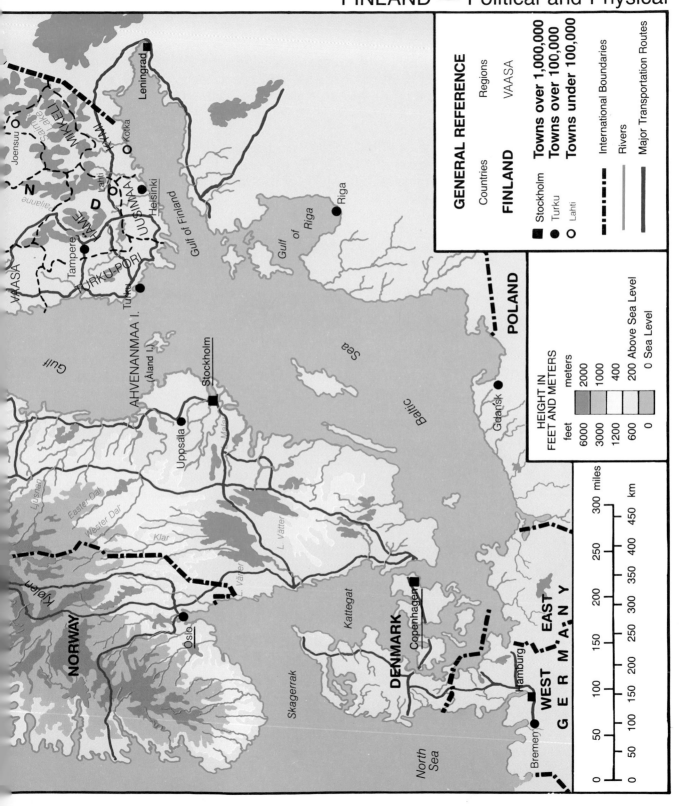

Leningrad

Kotka

Saimaa lake

Joensuu

MIKKELI

KYMI

N

Lahti

D

KUOPIO

Vanajavesi

HAME

Tampere

UUSIMAA

Helsinki

TURKU-PORI

Turku

VAASA

Gulf of Finland

Riga

Gulf of Riga

Gulf

Baltic Sea

POLAND

Gdansk

AHVENANMAA I.
(Åland I.)

Stockholm

Uppsala

Mälar

L. Ljusnan

Easter Dal

Wester Dal

Klar

L. Vätter

L. Väter

NORWAY

Kjölen

Oslo

Skagerrak

Kattegat

DENMARK

Copenhagen

Hamburg

WEST
GERMANY

EAST

Bremen

North
Sea

0	50	100	150	200	250	300 miles
0	50	100	150	200	250	300	350	400	450 km

Land

Finland is the most northern country in Europe. It is bordered on the west by Sweden and Norway, on the east by the USSR. The southern border is the Baltic Sea and the northern border is the Arctic. The northernmost 25% of Finland extends well into the Arctic Circle. Finland has an area of 130,119 sq miles (338,000 sq km), slightly smaller than Montana.

Finland has more than 60,000 lakes and 30,000 coastal islands. These lakes are quite shallow. Because shallow water can be easily polluted, Finns have a strong interest in preserving the purity of their lakes. Much of the land has been set aside as nature preserves and national parkland.

Until 8,000 years ago, most of southern and central Finland was covered by the Baltic Sea. Today Finland is still growing as the sea retreats about four sq miles (10 sq km) every year.

Climate

Even though Finland is so far north, the climate is not as harsh as you might think. Winds from the west blow air warmed by the Gulf Stream to keep the temperatures from becoming much more severe than in areas that straddle the US-Canada border.

Finland's seasons are distinct: long, cold winters — longer and colder in the north — and warm, bright summers. In the deepest winter, the sun never clears the horizon in the northern part of Finland. On the brightest of days, you can see a pink rim around the horizon. Snow falls from around Christmas to the end of March in the south, from mid September to late April in Lapland. The blanket of snow helps brighten the dark winter days.

In summer, the sun never sets in the north. This nightless summer lasts more than 70 days. This is long enough for the land to become lush and productive. Wild berries and mushrooms fill the forests and fields throughout the country. Many people grow vegetable gardens.

Agriculture, Industry, and Natural Resources

After World War II Finland had to repay the USSR for damage it had done during the war. At the time, Finnish industry was not very highly developed. But Finns hate to owe money, and the industry that developed to pay the war debt has carried Finland into the last half of the 20th century in fine form. Finnish industry is well known for the high quality of its products. Where many economically developing countries such as South Korea and China specialize in mass production, Finnish industry is known for products designed and made to order.

Finland supplies its own needs in dairy products, meat, and, in good harvest years, grain. Finland grows potatoes and other produce, but it must import large amounts of fruits and vegetables. Farms in Finland are small, but they usually have lots of timber that improve farmers' winter earnings.

Over 70% of Finland is forest land, and wood industries are very important to the economy.

Shopping at the open market at South Harbor, Helsinki.

Pulp and paper, construction materials, and furniture are the main industries. Over 80% of what the forest industries produce is sent to foreign countries, providing nearly half of Finland's export earnings. Finland supplies 10% of the world's needs in forest products. Related to the forest industry is the manufacturing of forest industry machinery. Finnish engineering workshops have supplied about 20% of the world's paper-making machines.

Heavy industry is powered by hydroelectric power. Hydroelectrically-powered plants produce lumber-cutting machines, spinning machines, cruise ships, ice-breaking ships, construction cranes, oil rigs, electric generators, and cables. Many of these machines and ships are exported. Finnish ships are common in the Gulf waters of Mexico and the southern US, often flying Norwegian flags.

Especially important to the economy are exports of chemicals, textiles, and arts and crafts. Marimekko and Fiskars are Finnish companies that now have manufacturing plants in the US. Marimekko makes textiles, especially clothes and bed linens. Fiskars is known for the high quality of its knives and scissors.

Finland has a variety of minerals, but they do not contribute very much to the economy because they are being depleted. Finland's 10 operating mines will likely be closed by 1990. Two are iron ore mines. Other minerals are copper, nickel, zinc, chrome, and cobalt.

Sports and Recreation

Recreation

Finns take very seriously the need to have leisure time. All workers have at least four weeks of vacation a year. Most work places have facilities for recreation, so workers make exercise a part of their day. Every town, no matter how small, has a sports field that is used throughout the year.

Most Finns spend at least part of their summer in the country. Many have a summer cottage known as a *mökki*. Some of these places are just one room, or *tupa*, with a sauna near the water. Finns regard the peace and solitude of the forests and lakes as necessary for building character and finding contentment. Even Finns who live in the country often have another place to which they can retreat and where they can live more simply for a time. This tradition dates to the old days when the whole family, including grandparents, servants, and animals, moved to barn lofts for the annual cleaning of the house.

Sports

Sports in Finland are non-professional. Teams for all levels of skill exist in a wide variety of sports, and clubs and town recreation centers make sports available to everybody. Finland is not a country where sports are mainly for young men. Just as everybody must eat to grow and stay well, Finns believe everyone must have physical exercise to stay healthy.

Favorite summer sports include jogging, swimming, cycling, and soccer. The national sport is *pesäpallo,* or Finnish baseball. In pesäpallo the pitcher stands in front of the batter and throws the ball straight up in the air. As it comes down, the batter has to hit it and run.

Internationally Finns are known for their participation in motor sports. Young children build and race K-karts, small cars like go-carts. Children from six to fifteen take part in competitions throughout the country. Finnish rally and Formula I drivers are well known at racing tracks all over the world, including North America, where they have won races in Detroit and Toronto. In 1982, Keke Rosberg of Finland became the World Grand Prix champion.

The most popular sport in Finland is skiing. Finns learn to ski before they start school and continue long after retirement. The Finlandia Ski Marathon is a 75-km (46.5-mile) race between Hämeenlinna and Lahti. Over 13,000 skiers take part each year. Hockey and other forms of ice skating are also popular spectator and participant sports. Even in the summer Finns train for hockey at indoor rinks.

The Sauna — a Fact of Finnish Life

The *sauna,* or steam bathhouse, has always been part of Finnish life. Here in North America we associate the sauna with sports, and most saunas are located in sports facilities. In Finland the sauna has a much more important meaning. Ancient poetry portrays it as a holy place. Nature healers performed healing rituals there. Babies were born in saunas because the saunas were clean. While people in the rest of Europe were dousing themselves with perfumed oils to cover up the odors caused by not bathing, Finns were building and using saunas in the belief that being clean was necessary for good health.

The word *sauna* is one of few Finnish words to be recognized and used in many other languages. In earlier days, the sauna was always the first building the settlers constructed. Here they lived with their animals until they built the animal shed. After the animal shed they built their barns. Only then — last of all — did they build their own houses! Until then the whole family lived in the sauna. Here they nursed sick people, cured meat, and washed clothes. Even after their house was built, the sauna remained the spiritual center of the home.

The oldest saunas were dug out of the side of a hill 2,000 years ago. Today Finns can buy saunas that they can put together in a few hours. Every house has one, and even apartment buildings often have a sauna in every apartment. If not in each apartment, the buildings have saunas for every four apartments. Dinner guests are often invited to take saunas with their hosts. Children take saunas with their parents until they are responsible enough to be left alone safely with the hot stove.

Here is how a sauna works: Traditionally a wood fire was built in a stove in the sauna. The stove heated the bathhouse, often taking several hours. Today the stove may be electric. People taking a sauna pour water from a ladle onto the hot rocks to create steam. They then sit on the wooden benches built into the sides of the sauna, occasionally pouring water on themselves and whisking their skin with branches. Men and women take saunas together. Children, too. The heat from the sauna relaxes the muscles and the mind and purifies the skin.

After a sauna, people take either a cool shower or, if they are in the country, a swim in the lake. Even in winter, Finns find a plunge in cold water refreshing and invigorating. An old Finnish saying tells you just how important people think the sauna is: "If the sauna cannot help a man, death is near at hand."

Helsinki

Helsinki is a city with 485,600 people. The Russians made it the capital of Finland in 1812, when it had only about 4,000 people. It is a clean and bright city. The old part of the city is surrounded on three sides by water. Helsinki is a lively city all year round. In late summer every year, the Helsinki Festival offers all kinds of music, theater, films, and art fairs. Throughout the year, citizens of the city shop for fresh vegetables at the open market in the South Harbor.

Buildings in Finland have been traditionally made of wood. As a result, many towns have been destroyed many times over by fires. Only fortresses and churches were built of materials that would withstand fires — hard granite. Many of these buildings are in Helsinki. Most famous of them is the Helsinki Cathedral in Senate Square. Helsinki is also the site of buildings designed by its internationally known architects. The conference and concert center known as Finlandia Hall was designed by Alvaar Aalto.

Helsinki is a city of broad streets and low buildings. Like most Finnish cities it was built on a grid plan. Here in the US and Canada, where our cities are quite new and many grew after the advent of motor-powered transportation, we are used to wide streets. European cities traditionally have very narrow streets, however. Finland's cities have often been rebuilt after being destroyed by fires. Now, with wider streets, fires are less likely to spread. The houses often face inward, with their backs to the street and fronts to a common courtyard.

A view of Helsinki from the harbor.

Finns in North America

The first Finns to come to North America settled in Delaware in the 1600s. Another group came for the California gold rush in 1849. By 1892, more than 36,000 Finns had settled here, mostly in the upper midwestern states of Michigan, Minnesota, and Wisconsin. The climate and land of this area reminded them of their native Finland. Between 1900 and 1910, about 58,000 more Finns came and half of them settled around Lake Superior. Today this region is home to more than one-third of the Finns who have come here.

Finns who came to the United States and Canada tended to settle in areas where other Finns had come before. Partly they did this because they were looking for land like the one they had left. But mostly they settled with other Finns because their language is so different from that of other Europeans that they could not communicate with anyone except other Finns. Two-thirds of the Finns in the new land became farmers. Sometimes they worked in cities to save money to buy land. But as soon as they could they were in the country building first a sauna and then distinctly Finnish style barns and houses.

Glossary of Useful Finnish Terms

Hyvasti (hih-VAHS-tee) ...... good-bye
Kalevala (KAH-lay-vah-lah) .. the mythological and historical poem of Finland
        based on ancient folk songs and tales collected in
        the 19th century

Kiitos (KEE-ee-tos) .... thank you
kota (KOH-tah) .... a Lapp, or Sami, dwelling. It looks something like a
teepee. It is made from reindeer skins and is
portable, being taken from one place to another as
the Sami follow the reindeer herds.
mökki (MEH-kee) .... a summer home
Sami (SAW-mee) .... Laplanders or the Lappish language. In Finnish, the
Sami people are called Saamelaanen (SAH-meh-lie-
nen)
Sampo (SAHM-poh) .... an iron object forged by the mythical ironsmith
Ilmarinen; told about in the Kalevala
sauna (SOW-nah) .... a Finnish bathhouse where a wood or electric stove
heats rocks to warm the bathhouse
tupa (TOO-pah) .... traditionally a multi-purpose room. It was used for
cooking, baking, eating, weaving, sewing, tool-
making, repairs, and sleeping

More Books About Finland

Here are more books about Finland. If you are interested in any of them, check
your library. They may be helpful in doing research for the "Things to Do" projects
that follow.

Bobbi, Father of the Finnish White Tailed Deer. Sharp (Bobbi Enterprises)
Comet in Moominland. Jansson (Avon)
Finn Family Moomintroll. Jansson (Avon)
Land and People of Finland. Berry (Lippincott)
Land of Heroes: Re-Telling of the Kalevala. Synge (Macmillan)

Things to Do — Research Projects

Finland is a country that goes to great lengths to preserve its neutrality. As such, it
should be of great interest to students who want to learn more about how a
Western country keeps a stable relationship with a neighbor like the USSR. As you
read about Finland, keep in mind the importance of having current information.
That is why current newspapers and magazines are useful sources of information.
Two publications your library may have will tell you about recent magazine and
newspaper articles on many topics:

The Reader's Guide to Periodical Literature
Children's Magazine Guide

For accurate answers to questions about Finland today, look up *Finland* in these two
publications. They will lead you to the most up-to-date answers you can find.

1. For centuries Finland was important to the countries around it. Find out more about why. How did this affect its development as an independent country?

2. Finnish architects have designed many buildings in the US and Canada. Alvar Aalto and Eliel Saarinen are two of the best known. See if you can find out where their buildings are. Either visit the buildings if any are near you or find pictures in library books.

3. Find out more about the Sami, or Lapps, of northern Scandinavia and the USSR. As a minority group overlapping the borders of several countries, how is their situation different from one country to the next?

More Things to Do — Activities

These projects are designed to encourage you to think more about Finland. They offer ideas for interesting group or individual projects for school or home.

1. How far is Rovaniemi from where you live? Using maps, travel guides, travel agents, or any other resources you know of, find out how you can get there and how long it would take.

2. Compare the amount of sunlight in winter and summer where you live with the sunlight Finland gets.

3. If you would like a pen pal in Finland, write to these people:

International Pen Friends   Be sure to tell them what country you want
P.O. Box 65   your pen pal to be from. Also, include your
Brooklyn, New York 11229   full name, address, and age.

Index